KABOBS for KIDS

Janna DeVore

Photographs by Zac Williams

GIBBS SMITH
TO ENRICH AND INSPIRE HUMANKIND

For Emma,

who started helping me cook before she could count—
I couldn't ask for a sweeter or smarter accomplice in the kitchen

Manufactured in Shenzhen, China in May 2012 by Toppan

First Edition
16 15 14 13 12   5 4 3 2

Published by
Gibbs Smith
P.O. Box 667
Layton, Utah 84041

1.800.835.4993 orders
www.gibbs-smith.com

Designed by Katie Jennings

Gibbs Smith books are printed on either recycled, 100% post-consumer waste, FSC-certified papers or on paper produced from sustainable PEFC-certified forest/controlled wood source. Learn more at www.pefc.org.

Library of Congress Cataloging-in-Publication Data

DeVore, Janna.
  Kabobs for kids / Janna DeVore ; photographs by Zac Williams. — 1st ed.
     p. cm.
  ISBN 978-1-4236-0557-7
1. Skewer cooking. 2. Cookbooks. I. Title.
  TX834.D48 2012
  641.7'6—dc23
                        2011039878

Adult Introduction

Be sure your kids are comfortable with skewering safely before they go full speed ahead. When I was testing the recipes in this book, even my two-year-old could skewer fruit and cheese on a stick effectively and safely. Bamboo skewers work best and skewer most foods easily. If kabobs require grilling or cooking, soak the bamboo skewers in water for at least 1 hour before preparing. This prevents the wood from scorching or even starting on fire while cooking. If you are not comfortable having your kids skewer with bamboo or metal skewers, try chopsticks. They work well for most recipes and have less pointy tips.

Kid Introduction

Everything tastes better when served on a stick! And it's certainly more fun to eat meals you've skewered and designed by yourself. Before you make that first kabob, you'll want to remember to:

● Be creative. The recipes in this book can inspire you to come up with your own kabobs. Colorful foods and lots of variety make for beautiful presentations. Use your favorite foods to create unique kabobs. If you don't like one of the ingredients listed in a recipe, leave it out or use something you do like instead.

● Skewer carefully! If something doesn't slide right on, ask an adult for help so you don't push too hard and poke your hand. Sit down to thread your kabobs. Don't run around holding kabob sticks or poke your neighbor!

● Ask for permission. Always get a parent or adult's permission to try out a recipe. And make sure your adult is nearby to help with the Adult Prep section for things like chopping or slicing or using the oven.

● Read the whole recipe and get all the ingredients together before you start. That way, you'll know all the steps and have everything ready when you need it.

● If you come up with a fabulous kabob idea or make one of the recipes in this book, take a picture and send it to kabobs@jannadevore.com. Once a month, I'll feature a creation on my blog, jannadevore.com.

● Have fun!

CONTENTS

French Toast

- 6 to 8 slices prepared French toast
- 4 to 6 peaches, peeled and sliced
- powdered sugar, for dusting
- maple syrup, for dipping
- whipped cream, for dipping

Adult Prep

Make the French toast and cut it into strips.

Make Your Kabob

Fold over a French toast strip, then thread it onto a skewer. Thread on a peach slice. Repeat until skewer is full. Repeat for remaining kabobs. Sprinkle finished kabobs with powdered sugar and serve with a side of warmed maple syrup and/or whipped cream for dipping.

○━●┼●●●━ Makes 6 to 8

Apples to Oranges

- 4 apples
- 4 navel oranges
- lemon wedges

Adult Prep

Wash and core apples; cut into chunks. Peel oranges and separate into segments.

Kid Assembly

Thread apple and orange chunks onto skewers in any pattern you would like. Repeat for each kabob. Squeeze lemon wedges over the fruit kabobs before serving to keep apples from turning brown.

○—●●●●●— Makes 4

Waffle Stompers

- 4 to 6 prepared toaster or homemade waffles
- 2 pints strawberries
- 10 to 12 breakfast sausage links
- 1/2 cantaloupe, cut in chunks or balled

Adult **Prep**

Cut each waffle into triangles. Wash and stem the strawberries. Cook the sausage links and cut in half. Cut cantaloupe into chunks or use a melon baller to make balls.

Kid **Assembly**

Thread a waffle triangle onto a skewer, followed by a strawberry, a sausage link half, and a piece of cantaloupe. Repeat until skewer is full. Repeat for remaining kabobs.

Makes 6 to 8

Rainbow Sticks

- 16 to 20 red grapes
- 1 pint blueberries
- 3 to 4 kiwi
- 1/2 fresh pineapple
- 4 to 5 clementine oranges
- 1 pint raspberries

Adult Prep

Peel kiwi and cut into 1-inch chunks.
Cut pineapple into chunks.
Peel oranges and pull apart into sections.

Kid Assembly

Thread 2 grapes onto a skewer, followed by 3 blueberries, 1 kiwi chunk, 1 pineapple chunk, 2 clementine sections, and 3 raspberries. Repeat for remaining kabobs. As you make each kabob, thread fruit so it lines up equally on the sticks.

To serve, place skewers side by side on a plate or platter to make a rainbow.

Makes 10 to 12

Blueberry Flowers

- 6 mini blueberry muffins
- 12 brightly colored cupcake papers
- 1 pint blueberries

Adult Prep

Make blueberry muffins.

Kid Assembly

To make muffin flowers, flatten out cupcake papers. Place 2 cupcake papers on top of each other and pierce through with a skewer. Thread 1 muffin onto the top of the skewer, but do not let the skewer go all the way through the muffin. The papers will look like the petals.

Thread blueberries onto skewers below cupcake papers. Place the muffin flowers in a vase and arrange as desired.

○—●●●● Makes 6 muffin flowers

Caribbean Kabobs

- 3 to 4 kiwi
- 1/2 fresh pineapple
- 2 mangoes
- 1 cup vanilla-flavored Greek yogurt
- 2 tablespoons honey
- 1/4 teaspoon ground cinnamon

Adult Prep

Peel kiwi and cut into 1-inch chunks. Cut pineapple into chunks. Peel mangoes and cut into chunks. Combine yogurt, honey, and cinnamon in a small bowl and stir well.

Kid Assembly

Thread fruit onto skewer 1 piece at a time. Choose any pattern you would like. Repeat for each kabob. Serve kabobs with cinnamon-honey sauce for dipping.

○—●|●●●— Makes 6 to 8

Grilled Cheese on a Stick

- 4 prepared grilled cheese sandwiches

- 4 pickles

Adult Prep

Make grilled cheese sandwiches.

Kid Assembly

When grilled cheese sandwiches are slightly cooled, cut out fun shapes with cookie cutters. Thread on skewers. Top each with a pickle.

O—●●●●●—— Makes 4

Spinach Salad on a Stick

- 2 pints strawberries
- 1 bag spinach
- 3 mangoes
- 1/2 honeydew melon
- lime wedges
- poppy seed dressing*

*Brianna's Home Style Poppy Seed dressing is a good choice.

Adult Prep

Wash and stem strawberries. Peel mangoes and cut into chunks. Cut honeydew melon into chunks.

Kid Assembly

Stack and then fold over 4 or 5 spinach leaves. Thread spinach onto a skewer, followed by a strawberry and a mango chunk. Thread another spinach stack, then a honeydew melon chunk, then another spinach stack. Thread a mango chunk and then a strawberry. End with a spinach stack.

Squeeze lime wedges over the top of the salad stick. Serve with poppy seed dressing in individual bowls for dipping.

Makes 8 to 10

Pizza on a Stick

- 1 premade pizza crust*

- 6 to 8 mozzarella string cheese sticks

- 1 package pepperoni slices

- green or red bell peppers (optional)

- mushrooms (optional)

- olives (optional)

- marinara sauce, for dipping

*Boboli is a good choice.

Adult Prep

Cut the premade pizza crust into small triangles or wedges. Cut the mozzarella string cheese sticks into fourths. Cut the bell pepper into chunks, if using. Leave the mushrooms whole, if using.

Kid Assembly

Thread a wedge of pizza crust onto a skewer, followed by a short stack of pepperoni, a piece of string cheese, and, if using, one of each of the vegetables. Repeat until skewer is full. Repeat for each kabob.

Serve with a side of warmed marinara sauce for dipping.

Makes about 8

Wedge Salad on a Stick

- 1 large head iceberg lettuce
- 1 to 2 cucumbers
- 1 cup cherry tomatoes
- ranch dressing
- 3 to 4 slices bacon

Adult Prep

Cut head of lettuce into small wedges. Slice cucumbers into thick slices. Cook and crumble bacon.

Kid Assembly

Slide a lettuce wedge onto a skewer, followed by a cucumber slice and a cherry tomato. Repeat until skewer is full. Repeat for each kabob.

Before serving, drizzle ranch dressing over each kabob and sprinkle bacon crumbles over the top.

○━◆━■■●━ Makes 6 to 8

Caprese Salad on a Stick

- 1 (8-ounce) carton fresh mozzarella balls

- 1 large bunch fresh basil leaves

- 2 cups cherry or grape tomatoes

- balsamic vinegar

- extra virgin olive oil

- salt and pepper

Variation: For a different presentation, thread only one of each ingredient onto a toothpick. Repeat with 2 dozen toothpicks for mini caprese salad bites.

Adult Prep

Cut basil leaves into smaller pieces.

Kid Assembly

Thread a mozzarella ball onto a skewer, followed by 2 or 3 basil leaf pieces, and 1 cherry or grape tomato, repeat the pattern until skewer is full. Repeat for each kabob.

Place kabobs on a large plate. Drizzle vinegar and olive oil over the top. Sprinkle with salt and pepper and serve. If not serving immediately, refrigerate for up to 1 hour.

○──••▮••── Makes 6 to 8

Sandwich on a Stick

- 1 loaf of your favorite sandwich bread

- 1 package of your favorite lunchmeat, such as ham or turkey, or both

- 8 ounces of your favorite cheese

- 1 jar pickle chips

- 1 cup cherry tomatoes

Adult **Prep**

Cut the cheese into thick slices, and then cut slices into about 1½-inch square pieces.

Kid **Assembly**

Use a fun-shaped cookie cutter, such as a star, to cut out shapes from the slices of bread; set aside until ready to use. Divide the lunchmeat into slices and then fold over each slice twice, so it's shaped like a square.

To assemble each sandwich stick, thread a bread shape onto a skewer, followed by a piece of the folded lunchmeat, a piece of cheese, a tomato, a pickle slice, and a piece of bread. Repeat until skewer is full. Repeat for each kabob.

Makes 8 to 10

Quesadilla Kabobs

- 8 soft flour tortillas
- 2 cups shredded pepper jack cheese
- 1 pint cherry tomatoes
- sour cream
- salsa
- guacamole

Variation: Try using other favorite quesadilla fillings on your skewers, such as olives, shredded chicken, or bell pepper chunks.

Adult Prep

Make quesadillas with the flour tortillas and shredded jack cheese. When slightly cool, cut the quesadillas into wedges.

Kid Assembly

Thread 3 quesadilla wedges onto a skewer, then 2 cherry tomatoes, then 3 more quesadilla wedges. Repeat until skewer is full or until you have used the desired amount of quesadilla wedges. Repeat for each kabob. Serve with sour cream, salsa, and guacamole for dipping.

○━◦┼◦◦◦◦━ Makes 4

Totem Pole Tortellini

- 1 package frozen or refrigerated tortellini
- 1 jar green olives, drained
- 1 can black olives, drained
- grated Parmesan cheese, for sprinkling
- marinara sauce, for dipping

Adult Prep

Prepare the tortellini according to package directions. Allow it to cool slightly.

Kid Assembly

Thread the tortellini, alternating with olives, onto a skewer as desired. Repeat for remaining kabobs. Sprinkle with Parmesan cheese. Serve with a side of warmed marinara sauce for dipping.

○━◗▮▮◖━ **Makes 6 to 8**

The Cobb Kabob

- 1 head green leaf lettuce

- 1 to 2 cups cubed cooked chicken or ham

- 2 to 3 avocados

- 6 hard-boiled eggs

- ranch or blue cheese salad dressing

Adult Prep

Wash the lettuce, pat dry with paper towels, and separate the leaves. Hard boil the eggs, peel, and slice in half lengthwise. Cut the ham or chicken into cubes. Cut the avocado into cubes.

Kid Assembly

Fold a lettuce leaf into a 2- or 3-inch square and thread on skewer, followed by 1 chicken cube, 1 avocado cube, and another folded lettuce leaf. Repeat layers ending with a hard-boiled egg. Repeat for each kabob. Serve with Ranch or blue cheese dressing on the side.

○─●⫴●●●── **Makes 8 to 10**

Meatball Sandwich Kabobs

- 2 to 3 dozen frozen meatballs
- 4 split hoagie buns
- 8 ounces provolone cheese, sliced
- marinara sauce

Adult Prep

Cook meatballs according to package directions. Let cool until warm but not cold. Lay split hoagie buns on a baking sheet and top with sliced provolone cheese. Toast under the broiler until cheese is melted. Let cool slightly. Cut hoagie buns into quarters.

Kid Assembly

Thread a hoagie quarter onto a skewer, followed by a meatball. Repeat until skewer is full. Repeat for each kabob. Serve with warmed marinara sauce for dipping.

○━◖▮▮▮● Makes 8 to 10

Hawaiian Haystacks

- 1 cup cubed cooked ham
- 1/2 fresh pineapple
- cooked white rice
- soy sauce
- shredded coconut for topping, toasted

Adult Prep

Cut ham and pineapple into bite-sized chunks or cubes. Make 2 cups cooked white rice. Lightly toast coconut.

Kid Assembly

Thread a piece of ham onto a skewer, followed by a piece of pineapple, then a piece of chicken, then a piece of cheese. Repeat until skewer is full. Repeat for each kabob.

To serve, place a little cooked rice on a plate, top with a little soy sauce, and then top with your kabob. Sprinkle with coconut and serve with shredded carrots and any other toppings you would like.

○—•┤■●■— Makes 6 to 8

Gumbo Skewers

- 24 medium-sized cooked shrimp*

- 2 green bell peppers

- 4 fully cooked sausages**

- 2 red bell peppers

- 2 tablespoons olive oil

- $^1/_8$ to $^1/_4$ teaspoon Cajun seasoning***

*If shrimp are frozen,
   thaw before using.
**Johnsonville chicken sausage
   is a good choice.
***Zatarain's Creole Seasoning
   is a good choice.

Adult **Prep**

Place bamboo skewers in water and let them soak for at least 45 minutes. Cut bell peppers into 1-inch chunks. Cut sausage into 1-inch chunks.

Kid **Assembly**

When ready to prepare kabobs, remove skewers from water. Thread a shrimp onto a skewer, followed by a green bell pepper chunk, a sausage chunk, and a red bell pepper chunk. Repeat until skewer is full. Repeat for each kabob.

Lay kabobs on a baking sheet. Brush both sides of the kabobs with olive oil. Sprinkle half of the Cajun seasoning over the kabobs. Turn each kabob over and sprinkle with remaining seasoning. Have an adult help you place the baking sheet under your oven's broiler on high. Let kabobs broil for about 5 minutes. Have an adult remove kabobs and turn them over. Return kabobs to broiler and broil another 2 to 5 minutes.

○━●●●●●━ **Makes 6 to 8**

Birthday Cake Kabobs

- 1 pineapple, sliced into 1/2-inch slices
- 1 (10.75-ounce) frozen pound cake, thawed and sliced
- 1 (8-ounce) package cream cheese, softened
- 1 cup powdered sugar
- 1 cup heavy cream
- 1 lemon, zested and juiced
- 2 tablespoons pineapple juice
- 2 tablespoons granulated sugar
- sprinkles
- maraschino cherries

Adult Prep

Cut the pineapple slices into quarters. Cut the pound cake slices in half. Make frosting by mixing cream cheese and powdered sugar on medium speed until smooth. Add cream and whip on high speed until soft peaks form. Mix in lemon zest, lemon juice, pineapple juice, and sugar. Refrigerate until ready to assemble kabobs.

Kid Assembly

Spread frosting on one side of each cake slice. Top with sprinkles. Thread a pineapple slice on the skewer, followed by a frosted piece of cake (unfrosted side first) and another pineapple slice. Repeat with two more slices of cake and two more pineapple slices. Finish each kabob with a cherry on top.

○—●⊕●●●— Makes 6 to 8

Chocolate-Dipped Frozen Bananas

- 4 to 5 bananas

- 1 cup chopped nuts, such as peanuts or pecans

- 8 ounces semi-sweet chocolate

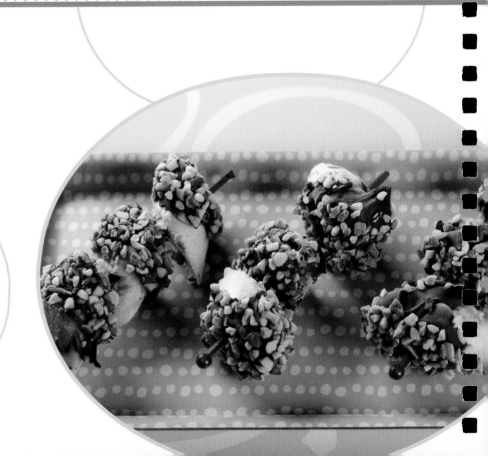

Adult Prep

Line a tray or platter with parchment paper and set aside. Peel bananas and slice into 1- to 2-inch chunks. Place chopped nuts in a shallow bowl and set aside. Melt chocolate by placing it in a microwave-safe bowl and heating for 1 minute on medium power. Remove from microwave and stir. Return chocolate to microwave and heat for another 30 seconds on medium power. Remove and stir until smooth. If chocolate is not yet melted, return to microwave in 15-second increments at medium power, stirring each time you remove it. Be very careful not to overheat the chocolate.

Kid Assembly

Dip a banana chunk into the melted chocolate to coat at least the top half. Then dip the chunk in the nuts. Set on the prepared tray. Repeat until all the banana chunks have been dipped in chocolate and nuts. Place dipped bananas in the freezer for 10 to 15 minutes to harden the chocolate. Remove bananas from freezer and thread onto skewers as desired. Return the finished kabobs to the tray and freeze for about an hour. Once frozen, kabobs can be moved to a plastic container with a lid and stored in the freezer for several weeks.

○━◆┃●●◆━ **Makes 6 to 8**

Chocolate-Strawberry Shortcake Sticks

- 8 ounces semi-sweet chocolate

- 4 ounces white chocolate

- 2 pints large strawberries

- 1 prepared angel food cake

Adult **Prep**

Line a tray or platter with parchment paper and set aside. Wash and stem strawberries. Cut angel food cake into $1^1/_2$-inch cubes. Melt semi-sweet chocolate by placing it in a microwave-safe bowl and heating for 1 minute on medium power. Remove from microwave and stir. Return chocolate to microwave and heat for another 30 seconds on medium power. Remove and stir until smooth. If chocolate is not yet melted, return to microwave in 15-second increments at medium power, stirring each time you remove it. Be very careful not to overheat the chocolate. Melt white chocolate by following above directions.

Kid **Assembly**

Dip a strawberry in the semi-sweet chocolate to coat. Set on prepared tray. Repeat for each strawberry. Dip a fork in the melted white chocolate and then drizzle each strawberry with white chocolate. Repeat with each berry. Let chocolate set at room temperature about 30 minutes. When chocolate is set, thread a berry onto a skewer, followed by a cake cube. Repeat until full. Repeat for remaining kabobs.

○━•┼●●•━ **Makes 8 to 10**

47

Caramel Apple Kabobs

- 1 package Kraft caramels, unwrapped
- 2 Granny Smith apples
- 2 Fuji or other red apples

Adult Prep

Unwrap caramels and place in a bowl. Microwave on high for 8 seconds to soften caramels. Cut Granny Smith apples in chunks. Cut Fuji or other red apples in chunks.

Kid Assembly

Make kabobs by threading a green apple chunk onto a skewer, followed by a caramel, followed by another green apple chunk, followed by another caramel. Repeat until skewer is full. Repeat to make skewers with red apple chunks and caramels.

○—•◦•◦◦•—— Makes 8 to 10

Fondue

- 2 pints strawberries

- 1 bag marshmallows*

- 1 bunch red or green grapes

- 1 fresh pineapple

- 9 ounces semi-sweet chocolate, broken into pieces**

- 3 ounces white chocolate or milk chocolate, broken into pieces**

- $1^1/_4$ cups cream

- 2 tablespoons butter

- 1 teaspoon vanilla

*Not mini marshmallows.
**A higher quality chocolate, such as Ghirardelli, is recommended for best fondue results.

Adult **Prep**

Wash and stem the strawberries. Wash the grapes. Cut the pineapple into chunks. To make the chocolate fondue, place both kinds of chocolate, cream, and butter in a microwave-safe bowl and heat for 30 seconds on high power. Remove from microwave and stir. Return chocolate mixture to microwave and heat for another 30 seconds on high power. Remove and stir until smooth. If chocolate is not yet melted, return to microwave in 30-second increments, stirring each time you remove it. Stir in vanilla. Keep the chocolate over a heat source, such as a warming plate or in a fondue pot, which will keep it warm but not hot, for dipping.

Kid **Assembly**

Thread a strawberry onto a skewer, followed by a marshmallow, a grape, and a pineapple chunk. Repeat pattern— or make your own—until skewer is full. Repeat for each kabob. Dip kabobs in fondue and enjoy!

 **Makes 8 to 10**

51

Cake Pops

- 1 box chocolate cake mix, prepared according to directions on box
- 1 (8-ounce) brick cream cheese, softened
- 2 cups powdered sugar
- $1/4$ cup butter, softened
- 1 tablespoon milk
- 1 teaspoon vanilla
- 1 package white almond bark or vanilla-flavored candy melts
- 1 package lavender candy melts*
- candy sprinkles**

*Or use another color you like.
**Try different holiday colors and themed sprinkles for different occasions.

Adult **Prep**

Bake the cake according to package directions. Let cool completely. In batches, crumble the cake into a food processor bowl and process until the cake is in fine crumbs. Transfer crumbs to a large bowl and set aside. In a medium bowl, beat cream cheese, powdered sugar, butter, milk, and vanilla until smooth and well combined. Spoon frosting into cake crumbs and combine well, using the back of wooden spoon or rubber spatula. Place, covered, in refrigerator until ready to make pops (up to 3 days if needed). Line a baking sheet or tray with parchment paper. When ready to make pops, melt almond bark and candy melts in separate bowls set over pots of simmering water. Stir each frequently and be careful not to let the water touch the bowls or let the almond bark or candy coating get too hot. Place sprinkles in small bowls.

Kid **Assembly**

Roll the chilled cake mixture into 1$^1/_2$-inch balls and place on prepared tray. Place tray in freezer for 30 minutes.

Remove cake balls from freezer. Spoon a cake ball into the white candy coating and turn to coat. Place coated cake ball back on tray. Sprinkle with candy sprinkles. Repeat with half of the cake balls. Dip the other half of the balls in lavender candy coating and sprinkle with candy sprinkles.

Let balls sit at room temperature until candy coating sets. You may freeze balls to harden but do not refrigerate. When candy is set, thread cake balls onto skewers or sucker sticks for a smaller presentation, as pictured here.

○—●┼●●●●— Makes about 8

Ships Ahoy!

- 1 cucumber, peeled
- 12 slices cheddar cheese
- 24 sword toothpicks

Adult Prep

Wash the cucumber and slice into thick rounds. Slice each round in half. Set aside. (These will be the ships.)

Slice the cheese into small squares, and then slice those to make right triangles. (These will be the ships' sails.)

Kid Assembly

Slide the cucumber, round side down, onto a sword toothpick. Slide the cheese, short side down, onto the toothpick. Leave a tiny bit of space between the cucumber (ship) and the cheese (sail). Repeat for each toothpick.

Makes about 24

Ballerina 'Bobs

- 24 blueberries
- 24 strawberries
- 24 purple or pink frilled cocktail toothpicks
- 1 tube decorating frosting

Adult Prep

Wash and stem the strawberries.

Kid Assembly

Slide a blueberry onto a frilled cocktail toothpick to just below the frill. Slide a strawberry, point side up, onto the toothpick. When held upright, the blueberry will look like a head with a feather hat, and the strawberry will look like a dress. Repeat for each toothpick. Use the tube frosting to pipe dots for eyes on the blueberries and, if desired, ruffles on the strawberry dress.

○–•◦◉◉●— Makes about 24

Ham and Cheese Minis

- 12 slices lunchmeat ham

- 1 (8-ounce) tub softened cream cheese

- 24 stick pretzels

Adult Prep

Cut lunchmeat slices into lengthwise strips.

Kid Assembly

Lay out 1 slice of lunchmeat. Spread with cream cheese. Wrap slice around pretzel stick several times. Repeat for each pretzel stick.

○━━━━ **Makes about 24**

Brownie-Berry Bites

- 12 brownie bites
- 1 pint raspberries
- 12 toothpicks

Adult Prep

Wash the raspberries.

Kid Assembly

Slide a raspberry to the end of a toothpick. Slide on a brownie bite so it touches the berry. Repeat for each toothpick.

○━•◦▪▪◦•━ **Makes 12**

S'more on a Stick

- 8 ounces semi-sweet chocolate chips
- 9 graham crackers
- 24 marshmallows
- 24 toothpicks

Adult **Prep**

Line a cookie sheet with parchment paper
and set aside. Place graham crackers in a
ziplock bag and crush with a rolling pin, or
crush in a food processor. Place in a shallow
bowl and set aside. Melt chocolate by placing
chocolate in a microwave-safe bowl and
heating for 1 minute on medium power.
Remove from microwave and stir. Return
chocolate to microwave and heat for another
30 seconds on medium power. Remove and
stir until smooth. If chocolate is not yet melted,
return to microwave in 15-second increments
at medium power, stirring each time you
remove it. Be very careful not to overheat
the chocolate.

Kid **Assembly**

Stick a marshmallow with a toothpick.
Dip and swirl it in the chocolate to cover.
Dip it in the graham cracker crumbs
and then place on prepared pan to set.
Repeat with each toothpick.

○━●┤●●●●━ **Makes 24**

About the Author

Janna DeVore is an editor, writer, and food enthusiast. She received her degree in journalism from Brigham Young University in 1997 and worked as an editor at a small publishing house in Salt Lake City, Utah, for seven years before starting her own editing and writing shop out of her home. She began experimenting in the kitchen at age eight, with the help of her mom and her local 4-H group. She is the author of *Ballerina Cookbook* and the editor of dozens of other cookbooks. She is excited to be on the other side of the desk now—even though writing a cookbook is much harder on the waistline than editing one! Janna and her husband, an officer in the United States Air Force, make their home wherever the Air Force sends them. They currently live along Florida's Emerald Coast with their four children.